PROGRESSIVE GREEK VOCABULARY
REVISED EDITION

With Mnemonic Method
Memorize Essential 365 Greek Words
Instantly as You Read

Students Say:

"Enjoyable learning experience."

"It works and it is difficult to forget."

"Just try one sample word if it works for you. If it does this book is for you."

"The only vocabulary book that you can actually enjoy to learn."

"Lol...that's what you get page after page while you remember all words."

PROGRESSIVE GREEK VOCABULARY:
Essential Words for Busy Pastors and Students
(Revised Edition)

"Developed with students like you and approved by the students just like you. The method is effective and always worked for my students. It is not like any taditional rote memorization tactic. It promotes a new and creative way of placing a Greek word image in your mind in an easy and creative way. Often you will experience that these words are in fact more difficult to forget after reading this book. It has worked for many students. See if it also works for you."

Progressive Greek Vocabulary:
Essential Words for Busy Pastors and Students
Revised Edition
Copyright © March 28, 2017 by Jason Jae-Cheon Jung

This book [PGV] is the second publication on the
Progressive Greek Series.

First Printing: May 22, 2014
Second Printing: March 2, 2015
Third Printing with Revised Edition: March 28, 2017
Printed by CreateSpace, an Amazon Publishing Company

All Greek words are from the Greek New Testament in
[NA27]. Nestle, Erwin, and Kurt Aland, et al., eds. *Novum
Testamentum Graece.* 27th ed. Stuttgart: German Bible
Society, 1993.

Cover Design: Lilian Jin and the Author
Interior Design: Lisa J.H. Roh
Illustrations: Ms. Jetoapple, *jetoapple@gmail.com*
Memory Tactics: Student Assistants like Adam Kent
                 who worked hard with the Author
Author and the Editor in Chief: Jason JC Jung

ISBN-13: 978-1545022757
ISBN-10: 1545022755
Printed in the United States of America

Special Thanks To

My students, who worked with me
for this work to see its bright light

and

Martin M.S. Lee
for financial support

TABLE OF CONTENTS

Your Commitment for Daily Study:

Date:

Signature:

Part I:
Seven
Basic Principles

1. How to Memorize

This book introduces several proven tactics for effective memorization. In all, effectiveness comes from a creative approach to learn a new word. Please consider the following example.

A. Words to Memorize
Let's say we have twelve words to memorize from number 13 to 24. With mnemonic method, these words will stick stronger to your memory, and will retain longer when they are attached to obscure memory aids as the followings.

13. **μισθός**, οῦ, ὁ – *pay, wages; recompense, reward*
    > "mistletoe" is a good <u>reward</u> for the fortunate
14. **σκανδαλίζω** – *I cause to stumble; I give offense to*
    > being "scandalous" can <u>cause sin</u>
15. **ἄρα** – *then, so, consequently, as a result; perhaps*
    > "A'r"ighty, <u>then</u>.
16. **ἄχρι**, ἄχρις – *until* (+ gen., or conj.) *as far as*
    > from beginning (ἀρχή) <u>until</u> (ἄχρι) the end
17. **ἔτος**, ους, τό – *year*
    > ἔτος μετα ἔτος = <u>year</u> after <u>year</u>
18. **παραλαμβανω** – *I take, take with/along; I take*
    > (παρα=with)+ "lamb"→ <u>take</u> a lamb <u>with</u>
19. **ἔμπροσθεν** – *before, in front of* (prep. + gen.); *in front*
    > "empress" comes <u>before</u> all
20. **ἔρημος**, ον – *isolated, desolate; wilderness*
    > nothing but "air" out here > <u>desolate</u>
21. **ποῦ** – *where? at which place? to what place?*
    > <u>where's</u> "Po?"
22. **κρατέω** – *I seize, control, rule; I attain; I hold*
    > "Karate" <u>rules</u>
23. **οὐκέτι** – *no longer, no more, no further; not*
    > "Oh kitty" no more!
24. **προσφέρω** – *I bring (to), offer; I present*
    > <u>I bring</u> my "ferret"

B. Visualize the Meaning

Imagine some awkward images in your mind, which either sound like the Greek words, or remind you of them. Students must take some time to build a mnemonic connection to each word in a creative way. For example, κρατέω (*I rule*) I imagine a guy in karate uniform hide behind the tree as above.

C. Store Securely in Your Brain

Important last step is to connect all images into a single storyline. Having a one full odd story in your mind helps increase retention rate for longer memorization. Then simply read the storyline several times while looking at the image. Those words will become ones very hard to forget even if you try to.

D. Extra Examples

New scientific research shows that human brain can neither be overloaded nor grow old. This means that the more you use it creatively it will become more effective. I have students in all ages from teenagers to retired pastors in their sixties, and the only difference in their performance on the vocabulary quiz is how creative the person is not how old he/she is. Just like any physical muscle, your brain can easily become tired with same dull functions. For this reason the more uncommon and odd images and stories you create longer those words are remembered better. See the following examples.

A picture may speak many words, at least twelve in our case. Be creative! If you cannot be creative gather friends in your class and do brainstorming. It will be actually more fun to work together to make words more memorable.

Pictures do not have to be beautiful. Stories do not have to make sense at all. In fact ugly pictures with awkward storyline is better for longer memory.

Give names to each character in your mental image, and be friendly with them. The more you feel comfortable with them they will be more accessible whenever you need them.

An imaginary picture in your mind may be
developed into a large scale storyline, which can be
conntected with another storyline(s). This will
actually create a drama or play in your mind, which
hold more as many words as your drama can play.

2. Noun Declension

A. English to Greek Declension

Charts and paradigms are indispensable for the study of Greek nouns, yet they are poor pedagogical tools when they are given to students with no instruction how to learn from them. No students are excited to study them; they are not like crossword puzzle that excites people.

The **noun declension** simply means a certain group or category of nouns showing similar patterns when they are inflected. Because the **inflection** is how a noun changes its form according to its function in a sentence, only knowing the basic form of a noun is sufficient for students to recognize its inflected forms.

Most students, who learn English as a second language, are enforced to memorize the English noun declension rules, before they come to an English speaking country. But when they actually arrive to that country it takes only short time before they realize that no native English speakers have memorized these declension charts. The natives know them naturally through frequent use rather than memorization. I believe this should be the approach to learn Greek declensions as well.

<u>**Noun Declensions**</u>

English	**Greek**
Number (Sg/Pl)	Gender (M, F, N) Number (Sg/Pl) Case (Nom, Gen, Dat, Acc, Voc)

B. Greek Declensions

The Greek noun declension is an artificial category that words are grouped under three classes that show similar patters when their words are inflected. The first two declensions have most of their words end in a vowel, while the third ends in a consonant.

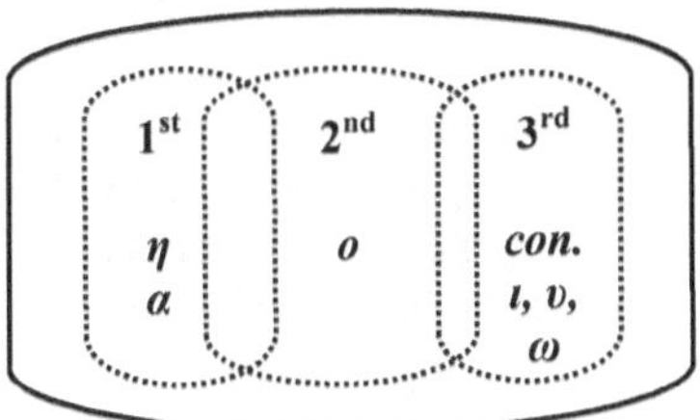

1. Noun stem ends in a vowel

Most first (1st) declension nouns are in the feminine gender, which ends in a vowel either in α or η. The words in the 1st declension tend to show a similar pattern when they are inflected for a different function (case). The second (2nd) declension nouns occur in two genders, masculine and neuter, which usually end in omicron o. For this reason the 2nd declension is often called an omicron declension, and there are more nouns in the 2nd declension than the other two declensions (1st & 3rd) combined.

2. Noun stem ends in a consonant

All three genders, masculine, feminine, and neuter, are found in the third (3rd) declension, and their stems usually end in a consonant. Many nouns do not quite fit into the first or second declension. These words are often wrongly accused as irregular or the third declension nouns. However, etymological and morphological examinations often prove they too have patterns in their peculiarities.
☞ Please see PGG, 78.

3. Noun Formations

A. Root > Stem > Word

The simplest form that carries the basic idea of a word is called **root**. For example, root for a noun λόγος and verb λέγω is λόγ and λέγ, which both carries a simple and vague idea of saying. However, when an *o* is attached to these roots each becomes noun **stem** λόγο and verb **stem** λέγο. They finally form **words** when they are combined with endings: a common nominative ending ς forms a noun λόγος (word) and since there is no verb ending for the first person active verb, λέγο becomes λέγω (I say) with the lengthening of the final vowel *o*.

B. Suffixes Forming Nouns

(cf. B. Metzger, *Lexical Aids*; PGG, 44-45)

1. The agent is indicated by -της.
- βαπτισ-τής (from βαπτίζω), one who baptizes
- μαθη-τής (μανθάνω), one who learns; disciple.

2. An action is indicated by -μος, -σις.
They often produce the abstract name for an action.
- βαπτισ-μός (βαπτίζω), a washing, purification
- δικαίω-σις (δικαιόω), justification

3. The result of an action is written by -μα.
- βαπτισ-μα (βαπτίζω), baptism
- γράμ-μα (γραφω), thing written, a letter
- κήρυγ-μα (κηρύσσω), preaching, heralding

4. The abstract idea of quality: -ια, -οτης, -συνη.
- σοφ-ία, wisdom
- σωτηρ-ία, salvation
- κυρι-στης, lordship, dominion
- ἀγαθω-σύνη, goodness
- δικαιο-σύνη, righteousness

C. Suffixes Forming Adjectives

(cf. B. Metzger, *Lexical Aids*; PGG, 45-46)

1. Adjectives from a Noun: -ιος or -ικος.

The meaning "of" or "belonging to" are formed by adding the suffix **-ιος** or **-ικος** to a noun stem.

- οὐράν-ιος, heavenly (from οὐραντός, heaven)
- πλούσ-ιος, wealthy (from πλοῦτος, wealth)
- τίμ-ιος, precious, honorable (from τιμή, honor)
- βασιλ-ικος, kingly, royal (from βασιλευς, king)
- σαρκ-ικός, fleshly, carnal (from σάρξ, flesh)

2. Adjectives with Verbal Force: -τος, -τεος

a. Verbal stem + -τος

It gives either a perfective passive participle or possibility particle in meaning. This formation is often seen in the classical Greek texts such as Lucian, Thucydides, Plato, as well as in the New Testament.

i) Perfective passive participle in meaning

- ἀγαπη-τός, beloved
- εὐλογη-τός, blessed
- νεόπλου-τος, suddenly-enriched
- κρθπ-τός, hidden

ii) Possibility participle in meaning

- ἀνεκ-τός, bearable, tolerable
- ἀδύνα-τός, impossible

b. Aorist passive verbal stem + -τέος, -τέᾱ, -τέον

When it expresses obligation or necessary

- λύτέοι οἱ κύνες, Dogs *must be loosed*
- ὠφελητέᾱ σοι ἡ τυφλὴ ἐστίν
- = The blind (lady, woman) must be helped for you.
- = You must help the blind lady.

4. Verb Examination

A. Verb Examination

The formation of a word indicates its function in the sentence. Examination of a verb requires three-step process. When you examine a Greek verb you should first look at the end of a word for its inflected meanings such as its person and number. Then look at the middle of the word if anything is inserted between the stem and the ending. This step will allow you to find out the tense, voice, and sometimes the mood of the word. Lastly, you should focus on the beginning of the word before you decide the final meaning of the word in the sentence.

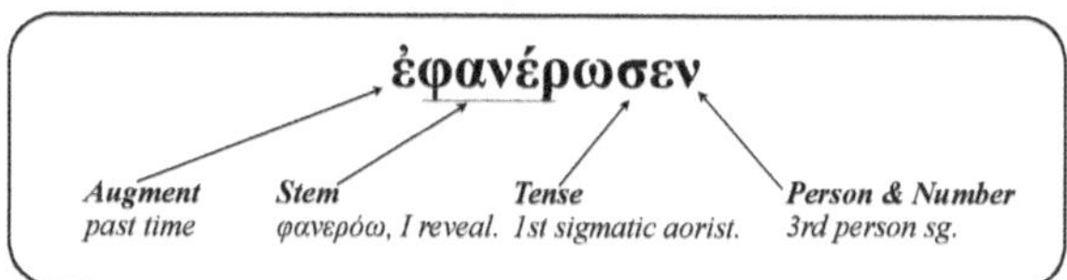

B. Comparison of the Formatives

Formatives	Tense/ Voice	Example
-σ	Future active, middle	παιδεύσομεν
-σα	Aorist active, middle	ἐμαίδευσα
-κα	Perfect active	πεπάιδευκα
-κει	Pluperfect active	ἐπεπαιδεύκειν
-θη	Aorist passive	ἐπαιδεύθημεν
-θησ	Future passive	παιδευθησόμενθα
--	Perfect mid, pass	πεπαίδευμαι
--	Pluperfect mid, pass	ἐπεπαιδεύμην

5. Verb Formations

A. Present Active Indicative Verb: λύω (cf. PGG, 40)
The most common paradigm word for Greek verb inflection is λύω. The full indicative paradigm for the present tense acting verb λύω gives five major information (T.V.M.P.N.) about this verb.

Singular		Plural	
I loose	λύ-ω	we loose	λύ-ομεν
you loose	λύ-εις	you loose	λύ-ετε
he looses	λύ-ει	they loose	λύ-ουσι(ν)

1. Stem: The stem of λύω is λύ- and the stem remains unchanged throughout the present tense indicative paradigm. The stem is the skeleton of a verb, which gives the uninflected definition, e.g. λυ- means "to loose." However, the stem is the second most fundamental part of a verb, because every verb has an unaltered core called the "root."

2. Voice: The voice for the indicative word λύω is active, and it has the active personal endings (--, -ες, -ι, -μεν, -τε, -νσι) attached to the stem λυ-. There are only four sets of six endings to learn, i.e. twenty-four endings with minor variations, for all Greek indicative verb endings. The six endings in the bracket are the one of those four sets.

3. Thematic Vowel: Most indicative words require connecting vowels (either omega *o*, or epsilon *e*) between the stem and the ending. This connecting vowel is grammatically called as a "thematic vowel," and the indicative verbs have two kinds of thematic vowels: *o*, *ε*. The thematic vowel omicron *o* is used when the personal ending begins with λ, π, μ, ν; all others use epsilon ε. All thematic indicative words have either o or ε between the stem and the ending. Thus, in case of λύω the thematic vowel is employed in the following order: o, ε, ε, o, ε, o.

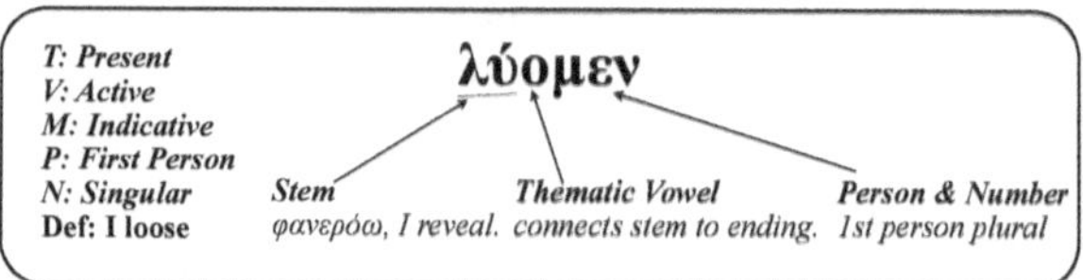

4. Vowel Contraction: When two vowels combine they are either shortened, lengthened, or altered. For example, the 2nd person singular λύω is the combination of λυ (stem) + ε (thematic vowel) + ες (personal ending). When the thematic vowel ε meets another ε in the ending ες, they are contracted as ε + ε > ει. Thus, λυ + ε + ες > λυ-εις > λύεις.

5. Personal Ending: In #2 above, the active personal endings are said to be --, -ες, -ι, -μεν, -τε, -νσι. However, the 1st person singular and the 3rd person plural do not show these endings. For the 1st person singular ending is the lengthend form of the thematic vowel o, which is omega ω for it cannot stand by itself at the end of a word.

For the 3rd person plural ending λύουσι the formation is that λύ (stem) + o (thematic vowel) + νσι (personal active ending), but nu ν, which is stuck in between o and σ is usually dropped due to a phonetic reason, i.e. to form more natural sound. However, when nu ν is dropped it leaves a mark that something has been dropped. Often the mark is the lengthening of the first vowel. Therefore, λύ + o + νσι > λύ + ου + σι > λύουσι(ν).

6. Movable *nu*: This last nu ν is called the movable nu, which is usually added to verbs that end with either ε or ι, but often (this means not always) removed when the following word begins with a consonant.

7. Variation of Forms: As discussed in #4 "vowel contraction" there can be variations in word endings. Most variations are simply phonetic adjustments to words in order to make sound natural or easier to speak.

8. Contract Verbs: The following indicative verbs are called contract verbs since their personal endings undergo contractions between the stem and thematic vowels: τιμάω, φιλέω, and δηλόω are typical examples.

B. Indicative Words: Form Division (PGG, 133f)
1. Non-thematic words
Most Greek indicatives have a thematic vowel (o or ε) attached after the stem. However, some words have their stem directly attached to their personal endings without a thematic vowel, and these words are called non-thematic or athematic words. They are primitive that some grammarians believe that all Greek words are originated from athematic words such as εἰμί, δίδωμι, and τίθημι.

2. Thematic words
The polarization of Hellenistic Greek has brought popularity to the Greek language in wider regions. Daily use of this *common* Greek has begun to implement thematic vowels (o and ε) in order to distinguish stems (meaning) from endings (functions). The basic rule for the thematic vowel is that a thematic vowel o before λ, π, μ, ν, otherwise, ε.

6. Greek Tenses

A. English Tense vs Greek Tense (PGG, 129)
Morphologically speaking, English has only two tenses: present and past. In English tense system, the ground for a verb lies on time element (past, present, future). The kind of an action is represented through eleven different aspects such as progressive perfective, imperfective, and they are expressed with primary verbs such as had, have, is, and was. Greek, on the other hand, has seven different tenses: present, future, perfect, future perfect, imperfect, aorist, pluperfect. In Greek, a single indicative verb can and does express both time and kind of action conveying the author's mind without the support of primary auxiliaries like in English.

B. Moods vs Tenses
Greek moods describe how the author (i.e. speaker or writer) considers his action from the standpoint of reality. Indicative mood denotes a verbal idea as actual in time present, past, or future. Imperartive writes an action with his volition; thus, the reality is *possible,* yet conditioned by the other's response. These two moods—the indicative and imperative—are the moods of the mouth for the author's mind is explicitly expressed.

There are two other moods that denote possibility and not actuality. The subjunctive and the optative mood are the moods of the mind for this reason. Accordingly, the subjuctive is called the mood of mild contingency, optative strong contingency. Moreover, some grammarians define each as the mood of probability and the mood of wish.

While the indicative mood concerns both "when" and "how" an action occurs, the other three moods (imperative, subjunctive, optative) solely concern for "how"—regardless of time—an acion occurs. Therefore in Greek, for example, the present and future tense have their time value only when verbs are written in the indicatives. Had an action written outside of the indicative mood, then the action has no value in time, because the other three moods only concern for "how" an action occurs.

C. Primary vs Secondary Tense

> **Primary**: *no augment, present & future in time*
> Active endings: --, -ς, -ι, -μεν, -τε, -νσι(ν)
> Mid/Passives: -μαι, -σαι, -ται, -μεθα, -σθε, -νται
>
> **Secondary**: *augmented, usually past, aspect focus*
> Active endings: -ν, -ς, --, -μεν, -τε, -ν (or -σαν)
> Mid/Passives: -μην, -σο, -το, -μεθα, -σθε, -ντο

D. What is the tense of that verb?

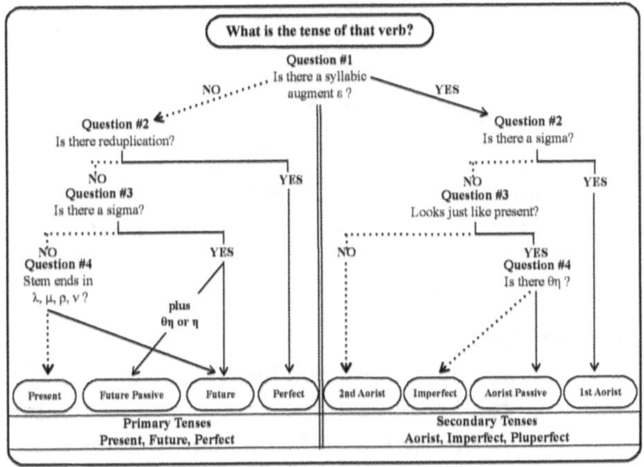

7. Moods and Voices

A. Philosophy of Greek Moods (PGG, 270ff)

In real life there tends to be more sensitive person than others in how things are said to the person. Thus, same truth can be expressed in various ways, and hearer is totally responsible to perceive the speaker's intentional meaning.

Grammatical "mood" differs only little from such illustration, since the Greek moods are concerned for both power and package of speaker's message. In other words, the mood informs the hearer/reader both verbal force (from simple wish to strong command) and verbal reality (from remote-impossible-unreal to possible-real).

B. Four Greek Moods

The Greek language has four grammatical moods: indicative, imperative, subjunctive, and optative. These moods can be distinctively positioned according to the two major categories: verbal force and verbal reality.

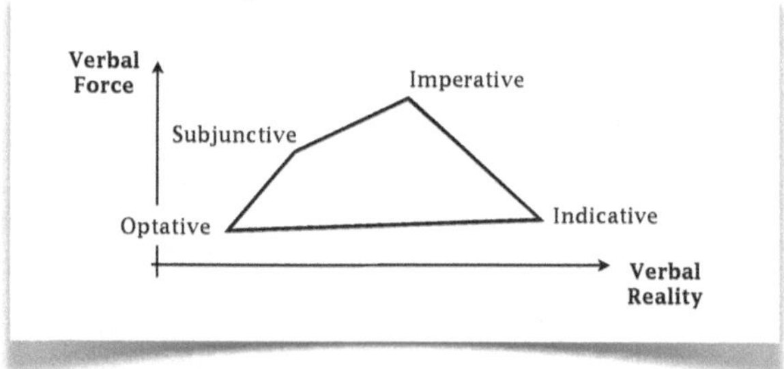

1. Verbal force

Regarding the verbal force the imperative and subjunctive tend to have more forceful reading than indicative and optative moods. The imperative in general expresses speaker's desire (expectation with intent) to change the attitude (action) of the audience (direct object). Subjunctive mood, which also has only present and aorist tense (rarely perfect), expects a certain event (action) to take place in the future. Its expectation is often conveyed in hortatory ("let us"), prohibition ("do not"), rhetoric (question), or fearing clause (with words such as φοβέομαι, κίνδυνος).

2. Verbal reality

As discussed above, the indicative and imperative strictly *deal with* the reality; however, the subjunctive and optative *concern for* the reality. In other words, in the subjunctive and optative, the verbal actions are not explicit in reality but only have potential qualities: the subjunctive is only one step away from the reality, but the optative shows two steps away from the reality expressing more remote desire.

C. Greek Voices (PGG, 107f)

English verbs have only two voices: active and passive. Greek has another voice in addition to these two, namely the middle voice. The middle voice is, however, a misnomer, because it sounds like denoting a "middle" voice between active and passive while it is not. Some attempted to explicate the middle as reflexive voice, but even that definition falls short in many instances. According to Robertson, the active voice is defined as "a word for another," passive, "a word by another." For middle voice, in the same regards, can be defined as "a word for oneself" according to the general understanding.

Part II:
Essential
Words
365

1. **φυλακή**, ῆς, ἡ – *guard, sentinel; prison*
   > "fool" I will "lock" you up, I'm a <u>guard</u>

2. **οὐαί** – *alas! woe!;* (as noun) calamity, a woe
   > Not (οὐ) "I" (αί) > not me > <u>Alas!</u>

3. **σταυρόω** – *I crucify; I fix stakes; I affix to the cross*
   > στάσις (standing) + ω (=verb sufx.) > <u>I crucify</u>

4. **ἀπαγγέλω** – *I announce, report, tell; I proclaim*
   > from (ἀπο) + an angel (ἀγγέλος) > <u>I announce</u>

5. **διώκω** – *I persecute; I pursue, run after, chase*
   > "Dio" (Spanish for God) <u>pursues</u> the lost

6. **θλῖψις**, εως, ἡ – *affliction, tribulation, trouble*
   > "eclipse" of persecution

7. **ναός**, οῦ, ὁ – *temple*
   > the "house" of God is a <u>temple</u>

8. **πλανάω** – *I lead astray, mislead, deceive*
   > a "plan" to <u>deceive</u>

9. **πρόβατον**, ου, τό – *sheep*
   > "robots" eating <u>sheep</u>

10. **μάρτυς**, υπος, ὁ – *witness*
    > "<u>martyr</u>"

11. **πλήν** – *but, however, only* (conj.)*;* *except* (+ gen.)
    > better to fly <u>except</u> "plane" is expensive

12. **προσκαλέω** – *I summon, call to oneself, invite*
    > <u>I "call" on</u> the "pros"

<u>Study Notes</u>

1. **μισθός**, οῦ, ὁ – *pay, wages; recompense, reward*
   > "mistletoe" is a good <u>reward</u> for the fortunate

2. **σκανδαλίζω** – *I cause to stumble; I give offense to*
   > being "scandalous" can <u>cause sin</u>

3. **ἄρα** – *then, so, consequently, as a result; perhaps*
   > "A'r"ighty, <u>then</u>.

4. **ἄχρι**, ἄχρις – *until* (+ gen., or conj.) *as far as*
   > from beginning (ἀρχή) <u>until</u> (ἄχρι) the end

5. **ἔτος**, ους, τό – *year*
   > ἔτος μετα ἔτος = <u>year</u> after <u>year</u>

6. **παραλαμβανω** – *I take, take with/along; I take*
   > (παρα=with)+ "lamb"→ <u>take </u>a lamb <u>with</u>

7. **ἔμπροσθεν** – *before, in front of* (prep. + gen.); *in front*
   > "empress" comes <u>before</u> all

8. **ἔρημος**, ον – *isolated, desolate; wilderness*
   > nothing but "air" out here > <u>desolate</u>

9. **ποῦ** – *where? at which place? to what place?*
   > <u>where's</u> "Po?"

10. **κρατέω** – *I seize, control, rule; I attain; I hold*
    > "Karate" <u>rules</u>

11. **οὐκέτι** – *no longer, no more, no further; not*
    > "Oh kitty" no more!

12. **προσφέρω** – *I bring (to), offer; I present*
    > <u>I bring</u> my "ferret"

<u>Study Notes</u>

36/329

1. **κἀγώ** − *and I, but I; I also; I in particular; if I*
   > <u>and I</u> am just another "cog" in the system

2. **σπέρμα**, ατος, τό − *seed; posterity, descendants*
   > "sperm" <u>seed</u>

3. **παρρησία**, ας, ἡ − *boldness, confidence; openness*
   > to ask for a "parley" is <u>bold</u>

4. **ἴδε** − *look! see! Take notice*
   > <u>Look,</u> idiot!

5. **πόθεν** − *from where?; how, why, in what way?*
   > this "potion" came <u>from where?</u>

6. **ἀληθινός**, ή, όν − *true, trustworthy; genuine, real*
   > "all ethi"cs come from <u>truth</u>

7. **κώμη**, ης, ἡ – *village, small town*
   > a "comb" is a <u>village</u> of bees

8. **καθίζω** – (trans.) *I seat, set, cause to sit down*
   > In "cathe"dral parents <u>sit</u> their little children quietly

9. **μικρός**, ά, όν – *little, small, short; insignificant*
   > "micro"

10. **φωνέω** – *I call (out), speak loudly; I summon, invite*
   > "phone me" > <u>I call</u>

11. **ἐκεῖθεν** – *from there*
   > "okay, then," we'll work <u>from there</u>

12. **ποτήριον**, ου, τό – *cup*
   > don't put your "posterior" on a <u>cup</u>

<u>Study Notes</u>

48/317

1. **ἀποδίδωμι** – *I give out; I render, reward; I pay*
   > <u>I render</u> "a pony" over to you

2. **κρίσις**, εως, ἡ – *(act of) judging, judgment; court*
   > during a "crisis" there must be a <u>judgment</u>

3. **φόβος**, ου, ὁ – *fear, terror, fright; reverence, respect*
   > "phobia" = <u>fear</u> of

4. **σωτηρία**, ας, ἡ – *salvation; deliverance; preservation*
   > "soterio"logy = study of <u>salvation</u>

5. **σεαυτοῦ**, ῆς – *yourself*
   > <u>yourself</u> breaths out "CO_2" (carbon dioxide)

6. **ἐγγίζω** – *I come/draw near, approach*
   > <u>I approach</u> "a geezer"

7. **ἐργάζομαι** – *I work; I do, accomplish, carry out*
   > "Hey, guys!" Come help me <u>accomplish</u> this!

8. **τιμή**, ῆς, ἡ – *price, value; honor, reverence*
   > "Team"play was <u>honor</u>able

9. **τέλος**, ους, τό – *end, termination, cessation; close, conclusion*
   > "tell us" how it will <u>end</u> (conclusion)

10. **πράσσω** – *I do, accomplish; I practice: I act, behave*
    > *whatever you <u>do</u> will be "plus" to the kingdom*

11. **ἐπιθυμία**, ας, ἡ – *craving, (strong) desire, longing; lust*
    > a strong <u>desire</u> goes "through me"

12. **ὑποτάσσω** – *I subject, subordinate*
    > using a "lasso" <u>I subject</u> an animal

<u>Study Notes</u>

1. **ἄρχων**, οντος, ὁ – *ruler, lord, prince; leader, official*
   > mon"arch" = <u>ruler</u>

2. **ὀργή**, ῆς, ἡ – *wrath, anger*
   > "ὀργή" of God is to leave people hanging

3. **ὀφείλω** – *I owe, am indebted to; I am obligated*
   > I "failed" to pay, so <u>I owe</u> money

4. **ἐγγύς** – *near, close*
   > an "angry goose" is waling <u>close</u> to me

5. **σκότος**, ους, τό – *darkness, gloom*
   > bats "scuttle" into <u>darkness</u>

6. **συνείδησις**, εως, ἡ – *conscience; awareness*
   > be <u>aware</u> to enjoy a "sunny day"

7. **διάκονος**, ου, ὁ/ἡ – *agent, intermediary; assistant*
   > "deacon" = <u>helper</u> or <u>assistant</u>

8. **μάχαιρα**, ης, ἡ – *sword, dagger*
   > "machete" = <u>sword</u>

9. **τελέω** – *I finish, complete, bring to an end; I fulfill*
   > Cf. τέλος

10. **ἐνδύω** – *I dress, clothe, put on*
    > <u>I dress</u> "into" some clothing

11. **κρίμα**, ατος, τό – *dispute, lawsuit; decision, decree*
    > "creamer" or not? This <u>dispute</u> will take a while

12. **θηρίον**, ου, τό – *animal, beast*
    > "three lions" > <u>beasts</u>

<u>Study Notes</u>

72/293

1. **ὅμοιος**, οἵα, οιον − *like, similar, of the same nature*
   > "homo" = <u>same</u>

2. **ἐπιγινώσκω** − *I know* (= γινώσκω); *I know; I learn*
   > ἐπι (against, on) + "no school" to <u>learn</u>

3. **κατοικέω** − *I live, dwell, inhabit, reside*
   > my "cat toy" <u>lives</u> in my toy box

4. **ἁμαρτάνω** − *I sin*
   > <u>I sin</u> if I drink "a martini"

5. **δεύτερος**, α, ον − *second; for a second time*
   > "Deut"eronomy = <u>second</u> law

6. **δέω** − *I bind, tie*
   > with "deo"dorant I <u>bind</u> myself with s nice scent

7. **διέρχομαι** – *I go/pass (through), travel, penetrate*
   > <u>Go</u> "Diego" Go! (from Dora the Explorer)

8. **ἐφή** – *he/she/it was saying* (or: … *said*)
   > anything <u>said</u> in the past is "ephe"meral

9. **θαυμάζω** – *I marvel, wonder (at); I admire, respect*
   > "theos" (God) is "<u>mar</u>"velous and <u>awe</u>"some"

10. **τέσσαρες** – *four*
    > "tessellate" square blocks

11. **ἑτοιμάζω** – *I prepare, put/keep in readiness*
    > "Hey" there's "Toy" R Us. <u>Prepare</u> to stop!

12. **μαρτυρία**, ας, ἡ – *testimony, witness*
    > Cf. μάρτυς

<u>Study Notes</u>

84/281

1. **οἶνος**, ου, ὁ – *wine, juice from the grape*
   > Buenos Aires is famous for its <u>wine</u>

2. **ἐκπορεύομαι** – *I go (out), proceed*
   > (ek=out)→"parade" <u>goes</u>

3. **ἥλιος**, ου, ὁ – *sun*
   > "helio"-centric = <u>sun</u>-centered

4. **ἀρνίον**, ου, τό – *lambs, sheep*
   > <u>lambs</u> "are neon"

5. **ἰσχυρός**, ά, όν – *strong; loud, mighty, severe, violent*
   > "it's cool," those guys are strong

6. **καθαρός**, ά, όν – *pure, clean, innocent, sin free*
   > "catheters" must be clean

7. **λευκός**, ή, όν – *white; bright, shining, gleaming*
   > "leuko"cytes are white blood cells.

8. **πορνεία**, ασ, ἡ – *immorality, fornication, prostitution*
   > "porn" is <u>immoral</u>

9. **θεραπεύω** – *I heal, restore*
   > "therapeutic" = <u>heal</u>

10. **ἀνάστασις**, εως, ἡ – *resurrection; rise (up)*
    > ανα (up) + στασις (rise) = <u>resurrection</u>

11. **εὐλογέω** – *I bless; praise; I provide with benefits*
    > "eulogy" of praise

12. **καινός**, ή, όν – *new; unused; unknown, strange*
    > I "kinda" know = <u>unknown</u>

<u>Study Notes</u>

96/269

1. **λύω** – *I loose, set free, untie; I destroy, abolish*
   > "loose" my tie

2. **μέρος**, ους, τό – *part; share; place*
   > good "merit" is <u>part</u> of sanctification

3. **ἄξιος**, ια, ον – *worthy, fit, deserving; corresponding*
   > My godly "si"ster <u>deserves</u> that "horse" as gift

4. **παρίστημι** – *I am present; I represent, offer, bring*
   > <u>I am present</u> "to stay" at the "party"

5. **σήμερον** – *today*
   > Don't say cheese but say "melon" <u>today</u>

6. **κλαίω** – *I weep, cry*
   > (bad German accent) "klying" = <u>crying</u>

7. **μισέω** – *I hate, detest; I disregard, disfavor*
   > I <u>hate</u> "miso" sauce

8. **μνημεῖον**, ου, τό – *monument, memorial; grave*
   > "monument"

9. **οἰκοδεομέω** – *I build; I strengthen, build up, edify*
   > "oiko"=house, "domain"=strong (<u>strengthen</u>)

10. **ὀλίγος**, η, ον – *few; little, small, short*
    > "Holy Ghost" never comes <u>short</u>

11. **θύρα**, ας, ἡ – *door; entrance, gateway, doorway*
    > he "thwack" the <u>door</u> as if it will listen

12. **καυχάομαι** – *I boast, glory, pride myself in, brag*
    > he "cackles" as <u>I brag</u>

<u>Study Notes</u>

1. **οὖς**, ὠτός, τό − *ear; hearing*
   > I <u>hear</u> a "moose"

2. **ποῖος**, α, ον − *what? which? what sort of?*
   > call "police"? For <u>what</u>?

3. **ὑπομονή**, ῆς, ἡ − *endurance, patience, perseverance*
   > "Mona" Lisa has <u>persevered</u> under ("υπο") time

4. **φαίνω** − *I shine, give light, am bright; I appear*
   > a "fine" <u>light</u> <u>appears</u>

5. **πλούσιος**, ία, ιον − *rich, wealthy; abound (in)*
   > a guy with a "flute" is "se"riously <u>rich</u>

6. **χώρα**, ας, ἡ − *country, region, district; field; place*
   > "coral" grows in a specific <u>place</u>

7. **φανερόω** – *I reveal, disclose, show, make known*
   > "funny" <u>reveals</u> character

8. **πάσχω** – *I suffer, endure/undergo (something)*
   > "Pascal" suffered greatly despite his brilliance

9. **λογίζομαι** – *I reckon, account, evaluate; consider*
   > "logic" <u>I reckon</u>

10. **ἅπτω** – *I kindle, ignite; I touch, take hold of, cling to*
    > you will "hop" when <u>I ignite</u> this

11. **δικαιόω** – *I justify, vindicate; I make free/pure*
    > "DiCaprio" justifies himself to be a godly man

12. **ἐπιτίθημι** – *I lay/put upon*
    > ἐπι (against, on) + <u>put</u> in your "teeth"

<u>Study Notes</u>

1. **περισσεύω** – *I abound, am rich, overflow*
   > the "police say" they <u>abound</u>

2. **εὐχαριστέω** – *I give thanks; I am thankful*
   > "eucharist" = thanks

3. **πειράζω** – *I tempt, test; I try; I attempt*
   > They <u>tempt</u> me to "pay" Mr. "Razo" for back pass

4. **πέντε** – *five*
   > "pent"agon = <u>five</u>

5. **βούλομαι** – *I wish, want, desire; I will, intend*
   > don't "boo" someone's <u>desire</u>

6. **διάβολος**, ου, ὁ – *devil, slanderer, adversary*
   > "Diablo" = devil

7. **διακονέω** – *I serve; I help; I minister*
   > "deacon" = I help

8. **ἐμαυτοῦ**, ῆς – *myself*
   > I call <u>myself</u> "Emma" "too"

9. **καλῶς** – *rightly; appropriately, in the right way*
   > to be "callous" is not <u>right</u>

10. **παραγίνομαι** – *I arrive, draw near, am present; I appear*
    > παρα (aside) + my "kin" are <u>present</u>

11. **ἀγρός**, οῦ, ὁ – *field, land, countryside*
    > "agri-"culture = <u>field/land</u>

12. **ἄρτι** – *now, just now; at once, immediately*
    > I want to see the "art" <u>now</u>

<u>Study Notes</u>

1. **ὁμοίως** – *likewise, so, similarly, in the same way*
   > Cf. ὅμοιος

2. **ἀληθής**, ές – *truthful, true, real, genuine*
   > Cf. ἀληθινός

3. **στέφανος**, ου, ὁ – *wreath, crown; prize, reward*
   > "Stephen" is King – <u>crown</u>

4. **πρό** – (+ gen.) *before*
   > "pro"active = <u>before</u>

5. **γενεά**, ᾶς, ἡ – *generation, contemporaries; age*
   > "<u>gen</u>"eration

6. **ἱκανός**, ή, όν – *competent, qualified, able; sufficient*
  > "I can" = <u>competent</u>

7. **εὐθέως** – *at once, immediately*
  > "you two" get here <u>immediately</u>

8. **ὀπίσω** – *after, behind*
  > to "appease" <u>after</u> is too late

9. **ἅπας**, ασα, αν – *all, the whole* (sg.) *altogether* (pl.)
  > "Hot Pass" works for <u>all</u> entrances

10. **βιβλίον**, ου, τό – *book, scroll; document*
  > "Bible" = <u>book/document</u>

11. **βλασφημέω**– *I slander, revile, defame*
  > "blasphemy" = <u>slander</u>

12. **διακονία**, ας, ἡ – *service, ministry; assignment; aid*
  > Cf. διακονέω

<u>Study Notes</u>

1. **διαθήκη**, ης, ἡ – *covenant, testament; compact*
   > "Do ya think" a <u>covenant</u> is not serious?

2. **ναί** – *yes, yea, truly, certainly, indeed*
   > "Nay" (does not mean <u>yes</u>)

3. **δυνατός**, ή, όν – *able, capable, powerful; it is possible*
   > "do not" not do what is <u>possible</u>

4. **ἐχθρός**, ά, όν – *hostile, ating; hated; enemy*
   > "EK! Throw" the <u>enemy</u> away!

5. **ἄνεμος**, ου, ὁ – *wind*
   > "anemic" people love <u>wind</u>

6. ἐλπίζω – *I hope, hope for; I expect*
    > "help is" on the way = <u>hope</u>

7. **καθαρίζω** – *I make clean, cleanse, purify*
    > "catheter" > <u>I clean</u> (notice ending)

8. **φλάσσω** – *I guard; I protect; I look out for, avoid*
    > Cf. φυλακή

9. **φυλή**, ῆς, ἡ – *tribe; nation, people*
    > "fools" at the Tower of Babel made <u>tribes</u>

10. **θυσία**, ας, ἡ – *sacrifice, offering*
    > a true <u>sacrifice</u> is "through" your life

11. **ἀσθενής**, ές – *sick, ill; weak*
    > Cf. ἀσθενέω

12. **ὀμνύω** – *I swear, take an oath*
    > when <u>I swear</u> (oath) it is "ominous"

<u>Study Notes</u>

156/209

1. **ἰσχύω** – *I am strong, have power, am competent*
   > "its cool," <u>I am strong</u>

2. **μυστήριον,** ου τό – *mystery, secret*
   > "<u>mystery</u>"

3. **νικάω** – *I conquer, overcome, vanquish, prevail*
   > "Nike" = <u>victory</u>

4. **προφητεύω** – *I prophesy, foretell*
   > "prophet" = <u>prophesy</u>

5. **βαστάζω** – *I bear, carry*
   > <u>I carry</u> the "bass"

6. **ἐλεέω** – *I have compassion/mercy/pity on/for*
   > Cf. ἔλεος

7. **καταργέω** – *I abolish, render ineffective/powerless*
   > κατα (under) + αργέω (unemployed) > <u>I abolish</u>

8. **πόσος**, η, ον – *how much, how many, how great?*
   > "puzzles?" <u>How many</u> pieces

9. **σός**, σή, σόν – *your, yours*
   > συ – "you"

10. **σταυρός**, οῦ, ὁ - *cross*
    > Cf. σταυρόω

11. **ἀδελφή**, ῆς, ἡ - *sister*
    > feminine gender of ἀδελφός

12. **ἀδικία**, ας, ἡ - *unrighteousness, iniquity*
    > leave the <u>evil</u> in the "attic"

<u>Study Notes</u>

1. **ἐπεί** – *since, when*
   > <u>When</u> is ἐπεί, then is τότε

2. **ἥκω** – *have come*
   >"hey, cool!" you <u>have come</u>!

3. **ἰάομαι** – *I heal*
   > "Yaow!" <u>Heal</u> me!

4. **λυπέω** – *I grieve*
   > ("loop"=circles) I <u>grieve</u> in circles

5. **ὁμολογέω** – *I confess, profess*
   > Cf. ὅμοιος + word > I <u>confess</u>

6. **οὔπω** – *not yet*
   > οὔ (<u>not</u>) + -πω (emphatic particle) > <u>not yet</u>

7. **πνευματικός**, ή, όν – *pertaining to the spirit, spiritual*
   > "pneumatics"mechanic use of pressure > Holy Spirit

8. **στρατιώτης**, ου, ὁ – *soldier*
   > "strategy tastes" good to a <u>soldier</u>

9. **συνίημι** – *I understand, comprehend, perceive*
   > "soon Amy" will <u>understand</u>

10. **φρονέω** – *I think, have in mind, care for*
    > <u>I think</u> I will grow a "fro"

11. **χήρα**, ας, ἡ – *widow*
    > true religion is to "care" for <u>widows</u>

12. **ἀδικέω** – *I wrong, treat unjustly; I do wrong, do evil*
    > Cf. ἀδικία = ἀ (not) + δικαιος

<u>Study Notes</u>

1. **ἀναβλέπω** – *I look up, regain sight*
   > (ἀνα = up) + I <u>see</u> a "blimp" > <u>I look up</u>

2. **γε** – *indeed, at least, seven.*
   > <u>indeed</u> he is "gay"

3. **γνωρίζω** – *I make known*
   > γνῶσις (knowledge) + ω (verb) > <u>I make known</u>

4. **δέκα** – *ten, 10*
   > a "deck of" cards has more than <u>ten</u>

5. **δένδρον**, ου, τό – *tree*
   > my "den" has no <u>tree</u>

6. **δουλεύω** – *I serve; I am enslaved*
> Let's "duel!" <u>I serve</u> you no longer!

7. **ἔνεκα**, ἔνεκεν – *because of, for the sake of*
> <u>for the sake of</u> "a neck"

8. **ἐορτή**, ῆς, ἡ – *feast*
> I'm "here ta" party! (= <u>feast</u>)

9. **κελεύω** – *I command, order*
> listen to my <u>command</u> or I "kill you"

10. **μανθάνω** – *I learn, found out, discover*
> <u>I found</u> a new "month on" the calendar

11. **μήποτε** – *lest, otherwise; whether, perhaps; never*
> <u>lest</u> "my potty" stops working

12. **νεφέλη**, ης, ἡ - *cloud*
> "nephilim" came from the <u>clouds</u> (Genesis 6)

<u>Study Notes</u>

1. **φιλέω** – *I love, like; I kiss*
   > Cf. φίλος

2. **ἀκοή**, ῆς, ἡ – *report, news; ear, hearing, listening*
   > noun form derived from ἀκούω

3. **ἀναιρέω** – *I kill, destroy; I condemn to death*
   > "anni"alate > destroy

4. **ἀσθένεια**, ας, ἡ - *weakness, illness*
   > Cf. ἀσθενέω = ἀ (not) + σθένεια

5. **διότι** – *because, for; therefore*
   > <u>because</u> it's a "d-o-t"

6. **ἐπιστολή**, ῆς, ἡ - *letter, epistle*
   > "epistle" = <u>letter</u>

7. **κεῖμαι** – *I lie, am laid; be, exist; stand*
 > "okay my" back is on the floor > <u>I lie</u>

8. **νοῦς**, νοός, ὁ - *mind, thought, reason; intention,*
 > need a "noose" for your <u>mind</u>?

9. **παῖς**, παδός, ὁ, ἡ - *servant, slave; child, boy, girl*
 > <u>servant/child</u>, "pass" the food

10. **παρουσία** ας, ἡ– *coming, arrival; presence*
 > he is <u>coming</u> to "peruse"

11. **πίμπλημι** – *I fill, end, fulfill*
 > <u>I fulfill</u> my hate for "pimples"

12. **σωτήρ**, ῆρος, ὁ - *savior*
 > "sootier"iology > study of salvation > savior

<u>Study Notes</u>

204/161

1. **ἀμπελών**, ῶνος, ὁ - *vineyard*
   > an "ample" amount of grapes are in <u>vineyards</u>

2. **ἀνάγω** – *I lead up, bring up; restore; put out to sea*
   > *ἀνα* - up & *ἀγώ* - I lead > <u>I lead up</u>

3. **ἀστήρ**, έρος, ὁ - *star*
   > "a stair" way to heaven > <u>star</u>

4. **αὐξάνω** – *I grow, increase*
   > our neighbor's sound increases

5. **γρηγορέω** – *I watch*
   > <u>I watch</u> "Gregorian" chanting

6. **εἰκων**, ονος, ἡ - *image, likeness, form, appearance*
   > "icon" > <u>image</u>

7. **ἐλεύθερος**, α, ον – *free, independent, free person*
   > Cf. ἔλεος

8. **ζῷον**, ου, τό – *living thing/being, animal*
   > "Zoe's" name means "living"

9. **θυσιαστήριον** – *altar*
   > Cf. θυσία

10. **κοπιάω** – *I have become tired or weary, labor*
    > it's a <u>struggle</u> to "cope"

11. **κωλύω** – *I hinder, prevent, forbid, restrain, withhold.*
    > I will not <u>hinder</u> a "coal" Christmas present

12. **μιμνῄσκομαι** – *I remember, keep in mind, think of.*
    > "mem"ory > <u>remember</u>

<u>Study Notes</u>

1. **ἀγοράζω** – *I buy, purchase, redeem*
   > "agora" = marketplace

2. **διδαχή**, ῆς, ἡ – *teaching, instruction, doctrine*
   > we <u>teach</u> to stay away from "the dark"

3. **συνέρχομαι** – *I assemble, gather; I travel with*
   > ερχομαι=come/go + συ=together > <u>I go together</u>

4. **γνῶσις**, εως, ἡ – *knowledge, what is known*
   > do you "know this" = <u>knowledge</u>

5. **ἔλεος**, ους, τό – *mercy, pity*
   > <u>mercy</u> will keep you from "hell"

6. **πάσχα**, τό – *Passover*
   > "πασχω"=I experience → the <u>Passover</u>

7. **ποτέ** – *at some time or other; once, formerly (past)*
   > everyone has to go "potty" <u>at some time</u>

8. **φεύγω** – *I flee, escape; I flee from, avoid, shun*
   > "fear go" → <u>flee</u>

9. **φίλος**,η, ον – *friend; loving, devoted*
   > "Phillus" is a great <u>friend</u>

10. **ἀγιάζω** – *I set part, sanctify, consecrate, dedicate*
    > (hick accent) "I guess" <u>sanctification</u> is cool

11. **γαμέω** – *I marry*
    > "game" over = <u>marriage</u>

12. **θυγάτηρ**, τρός, ἡ – *daughter*
    > θυ "γατηερ" = <u>daughter</u>

<u>Study Notes</u>

1. **ῥύομαι** – *I rescue, deliver*
   > a <u>rescue</u> never "ruins" a day

2. **πρωΐ** – *early, early in the morning, morning*
   > <u>prior to the morning</u>

3. **αὐλή, ῆς, ἡ** – *courtyard, palace, farm, house*
   > "outlet" mall in front of house

4. **ὀπίσω** – *behind (Mark 8:33); after (Mark 8:34)*
   > my "office" is <u>behind</u> this building

5. **κληρονομέω** – *I inherit, acquire, obtain, receive*
   > Cf. κλῆρος

6. **δῶρον, ου, τό** – *gift, present, offering*
   > a "dowry" is a <u>gift</u>

7. **βουλή**, ῆς, ἡ - *purpose, counsel, resolution, decision*
   > Cf. βούλομαι

8. **θάπτω** – *I bury*
   > "thop" (sound of dirt being put on a grave)

9. **ἀριθμός**, οῦ, ὁ - *number, total*
   > "arithm"atic > number

10. **ἀλλότριος**, α, ον – *belonging to another, strange*
    > there is "a lot" of a <u>stranger's belongings</u> in that "tree"

11. **θανατόω** – *to put to death, kill*
    > Cf. θυσία

12. **ἐνιαυτός**, οῦ, ὁ - *year, era*
    > Cf. ἔτος

<u>Study Notes</u>

240/125

1. **ἄφεσις, εως, ἡ** – *release, pardon, forgiveness*
   > noun form of ἀφίημι (I let go; forgive; discharge)

2. **συλλαμβάνω** – *I collect, gather; arrest*
   > συλ (together) + λαμβάνω (I take)

3. **ἀναστρέφω** – *I overturn, I behave, conduct myself*
   > turn "stripes" upside (ἀνα) down > I overturn

4. **ἄνομος, ον** – *lawless, wicked, gentile; criminal*
   > no (ἄ) more law > lawless

5. **συμβιβάζω** – *I bring together, reconcile; teach*
   > συμ (together) + βιβάζω (I exalt, bring up)

6. **ἀφορίζω** – *I separate, excommunicate, appoint*
   > "poli"ce separates "Joe" away

7. **ἄμωμος, ον** – *without blemish, blameless*
   > "no mode" of any mark left > markless > <u>blameless</u>

8. **ἐπαίρω** – *I lift up, I am in opposition*
   > <u>lift</u> up "Eiff"el Tower > <u>I lift up</u>

9. **ἐξίστημι** – *I confuse, lose my mind, am astonished*
   > "exoc"ism <u>loses</u> devil out of her <u>mind</u>

10. **ἐπιβάλλω** – *I throw over; put on; sew on; beat upon*
    > "balle"t on (surface of =) ice > <u>I throw</u> myself <u>over</u>

11. **ἀναπαύω** – *I cause to rest, give rest, refresh; I rest*
    > "power" to stop it going up (ἀνα) > <u>I stop to rest</u>

12. **παρουσία** – *presence; arrival; the Advent*
    > my "fa"ther, "See ya"

<u>Study Notes</u>

252/113

1. **νέος**, α, ον – *new, fresh, young*
   > "Nay" it's <u>new</u>

2. **πεινάω** – *I hunger, I am hungry*
   > "pain" in my stomach = <u>hunger</u>

3. **πάρα** – *on the other side; other side; across*
   > "part of" > <u>aside</u>

4. **περισσός**, ή, όν – *abundant*
   > "Paris" has an <u>abundance</u> of tourists

5. **σκεῦος**, ους, τό – *thing, object; vessel, jar, dish*
   > σκῆνος temple; σκεῦος temple <u>utensil</u>

6. **τελειόω** – *I complete, accomplish, make perfect, fulfill*
   > Cf. τέλος

7. **χαρίζομαι** – *I give freely, grant, cancel, remit, forgive*
   > he had the "charisma" of <u>forgiveness</u>

8. **δέομαι** – *I ask, beg, pray*
   > <u>pray</u> to "deo" (= God)

9. **δοκιμάζω** – *to put to the test, examine, approve*
   > the "doe key" is the only <u>approved</u> key

10. **ἐκλεκτός**, ή, όν – *elect, chosen*
    > the <u>elect</u> is "eclectic"

11. **θεάομαι** – *I see look at, behold, visit*
    > you will "say, oh my (lisp)" when you <u>behold</u> it

12. **καθεύδω** – *I sleep*
    > Wherever our "car stops" next we shall <u>sleep</u>

<u>Study Notes</u>

264/101

1. **καθίστημι** – *I let down*
   > "Kathy stay!" <u>I let down</u> my pet sloth

2. **κοιλία**, ας, ἡ – *body cavity, belly, stomach, womb*
   > your <u>stomach</u> is a "coil" of intestine

3. **πληγή**, τῆς, ἡ - *slow, stroke, plague, wound, bruise*
   > "<u>plague</u>"

4. **πλουτος**, ου, ὁ - *wealth, riches, abundance*
   > there are <u>riches</u> on "Pluto"

5. **πωλέω** – *I sell; be offered for sale or sold*
   > do not <u>sell</u> "polio"

6. **στρέφω** – *I turn, change, return; am converted*
   > <u>turn around</u> for another "strafe!"

7. **συνέδριον**, ου, τό – *Sanhedrin, council*
   > "<u>Sanhedrin</u>"

8. **χιλίαρχος**, ου, ὁ - *military tribune, high ranking officer*
   > leader (ἀρχος) of "Sili"con valley

9. **σε** – *as, like, about*
   > a metaphor is to "say," <u>like</u> or <u>as</u>

10. **ἀγνοέω** – *I do not know, I do not understand*
    > α (negation, <u>not</u>) + γνώσκω (<u>I know</u>)

11. **ἀντί** – *over against, instead of, for, in behalf of*
    > anti- (Eng.)

12. **ἀργύριον**, ου, τό – *silver, money*
    > "are you cool" with <u>silver</u>, "Rion"?

<u>Study Notes</u>

276/89

1. **τελώνης** – *tax collector, revenue officer*
   > <u>tax collectors</u> have "talons"

2. **τεσσαράκοντα** – *forty, 40*
   > Cf. τέσσαρες

3. **τιμάω** – *I set a price on, honor, revere*
   > "Tim"othy was <u>revered</u> by Paul

4. **χιλιάς**, άδος, ἡ – *a thousand, 1,000*
   > Cf. χιλίαρχος

5. **αἰτία**, ας, ἡ – *case, reason, charge, accusation*
   > there is a <u>reason</u> for this "idea"

6. **βάπτισμα**, ατος, τό – *dipping, washing, baptism*
    > "<u>baptism</u>"

7. **γονεύς**, έως, ὁ – *parent; parents*
    > Cf. γένος

8. **ἰχθύς**, ύος, ὁ – *fish*
    > "ick, this" is <u>fish</u>?

9. **μαρτύριον**, ου, τό – *testimony, proof*
    > Cf. μάρτυς

10. **νυνί** – *now*
    > "noon" is not always <u>now</u>

11. **ξύλον**, ου, τό – *wood, tree*
    > the "zoo" is made of <u>wood</u>

12. **σκηνή**, ῆς, ἡ – *tent, booth, dwelling, tabernacle*
    > <u>tents</u> aren't always "skinny"

<u>Study Notes</u>

288/77

1. **σοφός**, ἡ, όν – *skillful, wise, learned*
   > name "Sophia" stemmed from this

2. **ὑψόω** – *I lift up, raise high, exalt*
   > <u>raise</u> it "up so" <u>high</u>

3. **ὅδε**, ἥδε, τόδε – *this, such and such*
   > -δε points to things in certain distance

4. **πατάσσω** – *strike, hit, strike down, slay*
   > a hard "pat" is a <u>strike</u>

5. **σφόδρα** – *extremely, greatly, very (much)*
   > "SFO" (special forces officer) are <u>extreme!</u>

6. **πόλεμος**, ου, ὁ – *war, battle, fight, conflict, strife*
   > <u>conflict</u> happens "pole" to "pole" (north and south)

7. **πύλη**, ης, ἡ - *gate, door*
   > use the "pulley" to bring the <u>gate</u> up!

8. **ἰσχύς**, ύος, ἡ - *strength, might, power*
   > Cf. ἰσχυρός

9. **θυμός**, ους, τό – *anger, rage, wrath, passion*
   > "through most" people runs <u>passion</u>

10. **μήν**, μηνός, ὁ - *month, new moon*
    > "men" are born every <u>month</u>

11. **εἴκοσι** – *twenty, 20*
    > "A Course is" <u>twenty</u> dollars

12. **χρυσίον**, ου, τό – *gold, gold ornaments, jewelry*
    > he's "cruising" in <u>gold</u>

<u>Study Notes</u>

300/65

1. **κληρονομία**, ας, ἡ – *inheritance*
   > Cf. κλῆρος

2. **βοάω** – *I call, shout, cry out*
   > is that a <u>shouting</u> "boat?"

3. **κρύπτω** – *I hide, conceal, cover, keep secret*
   > a "crypt" <u>conceals</u> something

4. **μερίς**, ίοδος, ἡ – *portion*
   > Cf. μέρος

5. **κακία**, ας, ἡ – *wickedness, depravity*
   > hey that's my "car key" = stealing is <u>wickedness</u>

6. **δικαίωμα**, ατος, τό – *regulation, righteous deed*
   > Cf. δικαιόω

7. **ὕψιστος**, η, ον – *highest, the Most High*
    > Cf. ὑψόω

8. **θύω** – *I sacrifice, slaughter, kill, celebrate*
    > Cf. θυσία

9. **ἕξ** – *six*
    > eks > <u>six</u>

10. **πρωτόκος**, ον – *firstborn*
    > the "proto"type is the <u>first</u> > <u>first born</u>

11. **ἐπάνω** – *above, over, more than; over, above, on*
    > "up on" = <u>over</u>

12. **πρᾶγμα**, ατος, τό – *deed, thing, event, matter, affair*
    > "pragma"tics is all about <u>deed</u>

<u>Study Notes</u>

1. **μέλος**, ους, τό – *member, part, limb*
   > Cf. μέρος

2. **μήτε** – and not
   > "μη" = <u>not</u> …. "τε"/και= both/<u>and</u>

3. **πτωχός**, ή, όν – *poor, dependent on others for support*
   > "pity" for the <u>poor</u>

4. **ἀρνέομαι** – *I deny, repudiate, disown; I disregard*
   > "are never mine" = <u>disown</u>

5. **ἀσθενέω** – *I am weak/sick*
   > "thin" = <u>weak</u>

6. **ἱερεύς**, έως, ὁ – *priest*
   > "you're a" <u>priest</u>

7. **πλῆθος**, ους, τό – *multitude, large number; quantity*
   > "plethora" = <u>multitude</u>

8. **ἡγέομαι** – *I lead, guide; I think, consider, regard*
   > "Egg? Oh my!" <u>Lead</u> me to it!

9. **χρεία**, ας, ἡ – *need, what should be; lack, want*
   > "create" what I <u>need</u>

10. **χωρίς** – *without, apart from; separately*
    > a "chorus" is not <u>without</u> a group

11. **ὥσπερ** – *even as, just as*
    > ὡς (<u>as</u>) περ (emphatic) > just as

12. **δείκνυμι** – *I show, point out; I explain, prove*
    > "new to me" = <u>I show</u>

<u>Study Notes</u>

324/41

1. **εὐσέβεια, ας, ἡ** – *piety, godliness; godly acts*
   > "you say beyo"nd words > <u>godly acts</u>

2. **ἀρέσκω** – *I strive to please, please*
   > life is "a race" to <u>please</u>

3. **ἀόρατος** – *unseen, not seen, invisible*
   > ἀ (negation) + ὀρα- (to see) + τος (adj. maker)

4. **δεσμός, ους, ὁ** – *bond, fetter; bonds, imprisonment*
   > not many are "dismissed" from <u>bonds</u>

5. **προσφέρω** – *I bring (to), offer; I present*
   > towards (προσ) + I carry (φέρω) > <u>I present</u>

6. **προσκαλέω** – *I summon, call on, call to oneself, invite*
   > towards (προσ) + I call (καλέω) > <u>I summon</u>

7. **ἀποδίδωμι** – *I give out; I render, reward, recompense*
   > from (ἀπο) + I give (δίδωμι) > <u>I give out</u>

8. **ἐπιθυμία, ας, ἡ** – *craving, (strong) desire, longing*
   > a <u>desire</u> goes "through me"

9. **ἐπιγινώσκω** – *I know* (= γινώσκω); *I know exactly*
   > I am "happy" to have "no school" to <u>learn</u>

10. **κατοικέω** – *I live, dwell, inhabit, reside*
    > my "cat toy" <u>lives</u> in my toy box

11. **ἁμαρτάνω** – *I sin*
    > <u>I sin</u> if I drink "a martini"

12. **ἐκκόπτω** – *I cut off or down; remove; knock out*
    > ἐκ (<u>off</u>; <u>out</u>) + κόπτω (<u>I strike</u>, <u>hammer</u>, <u>smite</u>)

<u>Study Notes</u>

1. **ἄδικος, ον** – *unjust, dishonest, untrustworthy*
   > Cf. ἀδικία

2. **κέρας, ατος, τό** – *horn, corner, end*
   > I don't "care" about a <u>corner</u> of a Hebrew letter

3. **πλήρης, ες** – *filled, full, complete*
   > the light of "Polaris" (North Star) <u>fills</u> the sky

4. **ἀπώλεια, ας, ἡ** - *destruction, waste, ruin*
   > <u>destruction</u> is always "appall"ing

5. **ταράσσω** – *I stir up, disturb, unsettle, trouble, frighten*
   > there is always <u>trouble</u> near that "terrace"

6. **ῥάβδος, ου, ἡ** - *rod, staff, stick, scepter*
   > do not "rob" my <u>staff</u>

7. **λιμός, οῦ, ὁ** – *hunger, famine*
   > "limou"sines are always <u>hungry</u>

8. **ᾅδης, ου, ὁ** – *Hades, underworld, death*
   > "<u>Hades</u>"

9. **νεανίσκος, ου, ὁ** – *youth, young man, servant*
   > I'll put my fake "knee on" for the young to sit on

10. **πέτρα, ας, ἡ** – *service, worship*
    > "Peter" provided Jesus good <u>service</u>

11. **εὐλογία, ας, ἡ** – *praise, flattery, blessing*
    > Cf. εὐλογέω

12. **θλίβω** – *I press upon, oppress; I squeeze; I afflict*
    > "throw" the "bow" to <u>press</u>

<u>Study Notes</u>

348/17

1. **διοδεύω** – *I travel through, traverse*
   > "together" we may <u>travel through</u>

2. **εἴδωλον, ου, τό** – *image, idol*
   > "<u>idol</u>"

3. **δέησις, εως, ἡ** – *prayer, entreaty, petition*
   > all "days" should have <u>prayer</u>

4. **βρῶμα, ατος, τό** – *food*
   >"bro" got any <u>food?</u>

5. **ἐλεημοσύνη, ης, ἡ** – *kind deed, charitable giving*
   > "<u>alms</u>" giving will "soon" be "revealed"

6. **βίος, ου, ὁ** – *life, conduct, property*
   > "bio"logy is the study of <u>life</u>

7. **διάνοια, ας, ἡ** – *understanding, intelligence, conceit*
   > "do you know" the <u>purpose</u> of <u>understanding?</u>

8. **ἐλέγχω** – *I bring to light, expose, convince, reprove*
   > "a leg" of a woman should not be <u>exposed</u>

9. **αὔριον** – *tomorrow, next day, soon*
   > today is σήμερον tomorrow is αὔριον

10. **δεσπότης, ου, ὁ** – *lord, master, epistle*
    > "despotis"m (tyranny) is a political <u>master</u>

11. **ἕτοιμος, η, ον** – *ready, prepared*
    > "a toy" is always <u>ready</u>

12. **δόλος, ου, ὁ** – *deceit, treachery, cunning*
    > "dollars" seem to encourage <u>treachery</u>

<u>Study Notes</u>

365/0

1. **σπλαγχνίζομαι** – *I am moved with pity or compassion*
   > heart'll "spring" out for "my joy" > <u>compassionate</u>

2. **μιμέομαι** – *I imitate; I follow; I strive to resemble*
   > copycat was crying "memeo" to <u>resemble</u> my voice

3. **ὠρύομαι** – *I howl, roar*
   > 1 Peter 5:8 talks about a lion "ὠρύομαι"

4. **μετανοέω** – *I repent, undergo a change of mind*
   > μέτα (after) + νοέω (I perceive, observe) > <u>I repent</u>

5. **ἐπιτελέω** – *I bring to an end, finish, complete, perfect*
   > ἐπί (until) τελέω (I finish) > <u>I perfect, complete</u>

6. **βασιλεύω** – *I possess regal authority, I reign, rule*
   > "basilicas" are for <u>kings</u>

7. **γένος**, ους, τό – *race, descendant(s), family, nation*
   > Genome Project (dealing with new race)

8. **διδασκαλία**, ας, ἡ - *teaching, instruction*
   > Cf. διδαχή

9. **ἑκατοντάρχης**, ου, ὁ - *centurion, captain, officer*
   > an <u>officer</u> is like "a cat on tar"

10. **ἐκλέγομαι** – *I choose, select*
    > Cf. ἐκλεκτός

11. **ἐνεργέω** – *I work, I am at work, produce*
    > <u>work</u> produces "<u>energy</u>"

12. **εὐδοκέω** – *I am well pleased, consent, resolve, like*
    > "you do okay," <u>I am well pleased</u>

13. **ἐφίστημι** – *I stand by, appear, attack; I am present*
    > "A fist" is a <u>present</u> to <u>attack</u> you with

14. **θερίζω** – *I reap, harvest*
    > "there is" so much to <u>harvest</u>

15. **λατρεύω** – *I serve, worship*
    > you <u>worship</u> in a "latrine?"

16. **μνημονεύω** – *I remember, keep in mind, think of*
    > Cf. μιμνήσκομαι

17. **πειρασμός**, οῦ, ὁ - *test, trial, temptation, enticement*
    > a <u>trial</u> could be "peri"lous

<u>Study Notes</u>

Your Testimony for the Completion of the Study:

Date:

Signature:

PART III: SEVEN VOCABULARY INSIGHTS

I. Exercise

Practice makes it perfect. Now you should try to work with any new words in a similar fashion that has done in the previous section. Here are some sample words for exercises. Please create something memorable and unforgettable to learn these words.

A. Vocabulary Lists
Please first come up with a memorable phrase or sentence for each word below.
1. ποταμός, ου, ὁ – *river, stream*
2. ἑκατόν – *one hundred, 100*
3. τρόπος, ου, ὁ – *manner, way, way of life, conduct*
4. τίκτω – *I bear, give birth, bring forth*
5. κλῆρος, οῦ, ὁ – *lot, share*
6. πλησίον – *neighbor*
7. ὑψηλός, ή, όν – *high exalted, proud, haughty*
8. χρυσοῦς, ῆ, οῦν – *golden*
9. ἵππος, ου, ὁ – *horse, steed*
10. πληθύνω – *I increase, multiply; I grow*
11. κοιμάω – *I sleep, fall asleep, die*
12. ἔλαιον – *olive oil, oil*

B. Be Creative
Here are sample mnemonic phrases.
1. ποταμός, ου, ὁ – *river, stream*
    >the "Potomac" is a <u>river</u>
2. ἑκατόν – *one hundred, 100*
    >hectogram = 100 grams
3. τρόπος, ου, ὁ – *manner, way, way of life, conduct*
    >great <u>conduct</u> in life is awarded with a "trophy"
4. τίκτω – *I bear, give birth, bring forth*
    >you must "tip toe" around a woman <u>giving birth</u>
5. κλῆρος, οῦ, ὁ – *lot, share*
    >let's be "clear," this is my <u>share</u>

6. πλησίον – *neighbor*
>a child "plays" with his <u>neighbor</u>
7. ὑψηλός, ή, όν – *high exalted, proud, haughty*
>"hey, fellas" the <u>haughty</u> calling
8. χρυσοῦς, ῆ, οῦν – *golden*
><u>golden</u> opportunity often comes in "crisis"
9. ἵππος, ου, ὁ – *horse, steed*
>a "hippo" would make a terrible <u>horse</u>
10. πληθύνω – *I increase, multiply; I grow*
><u>increase</u> leads to a "pletho"ra
11. γαμέω – *I marry, enter the marriage state*
><u>I marry</u> so it is "game over"
12. ἔλαιον – *olive oil, oil*
>"I lie on" <u>oil</u> for my skin

C. Please sketch images for new words.
(please use the next page for more space)

D. Complie your pictures into a memorable story
(please use the next page for more space)

E. Now draw your story into your own picture
(please use the next page for more space)

☞ *F. Schaeffer once said that Christian was someone whose imgagination could go beyond the sky. Having creavity and building his imagination is believer's right.*

Exercise

Exercise Continued

II. God, Language, and Scripture

(Title from Moisés Silva's excellent title)

According to the current author's conviction, the very first principle of doing theology is to realize that God (θεός) is the subject and not the object of the study. Thus fundamentally speaking, theology is the study of what God (θεός) has to say (λέγω) for and of himself rather than about him as philosophy often does. For this reason, theology must begin and motivated from learning the Word of God as He is written in the Bible. This "Scriptural" theology is to give at least three essential knowledge: *who God is, what God does, how God relates to man.*

There is no better way to begin doing theology than to study the Bible from its original languages. But the first obstacle to read the Greek Bible would be not knowing Greek words. Thinking in Greek cannot be done unless its words are aquatinted.

As a theological example, it is helpful to consider how how faith in a believer works out for salvation. According to the doctrine of the perseverance of the saints whoever once believed Jesus Christ as his savior and Lord he will be saved from due condemnation. However, whatever the ones who have once believed but still lives in a worldly manner? Is it right for him to be saved as well as the others who work so hard for the growth of their faith? This controversial question finds a quick answer in the Greek New Testament. Simply there is no Bible verse, which guarantees salvation of once professed faith (except Mark 16:16), but it is always those (ὁ πιστεύων) who continually live out (present tense in Greek) their faith in daily lives who are saved. Even the one in Mark passage implies a believer (ὁ πιστεύσας) who has a strong enough faith to be baptized. Thus, his faith also denotes the kind of living faith that merits salvation.

It is a common mistake that the students's theology is often based on translations without consideration from the original text. Even many pastors with the basic knowledge of the Greek language often seem to judge Greek words according to their scale of English vocabulary. In other words, if the translated meaning of a Greek word is plain and simple in English the word in Greek too is often considered accordingly. It is a little exaggeration to emphasize again that the first theology is always a biblical one.

Short Bibliography (Title/Author)
Biblical Words and Their Meanig/ Silva
Devotions on the Greek New Testament/ Duvall
God, Language and Scripture/ Moisés Silva
God-Talk/ John Macquarrie
John Brown of Haddington/ Robert Mackenzie
Keep Your Greek/ Constantine Campbell
Language and Theology/ Gordon H. Clark
Semantics of New Testament Greek/ J. P. Louw
The Minister and His Greek NT/ Robertson
The Semantics of Biblical Language/ James Barr
Translating the Word of God/ Beekman & Callow
Understanding Language/ Donald Fairbairn
Using New Testament Greek in Ministry/ Black
When God Spoke Greek/ Timothy M. Law

III. Contextual vs. Lexical Meaning

A. Hebrews 11:1

Two similar words appear in this verse. Ὑπόστασις is used five times in the New Testament including three times used in Hebrews (1:3, 3:14, 11:1). While its verb form (ἐλέγχω) is common in the NT the noun ἔλεγχος is a hapax legomenon. NT writers save Paul and Luke tend to avoid such philosophically packed words, but when they are used it is safe to assume intentional. While the semantical range of ὑπόστασις varies as confidence, realization, or assurance, the meaning of ἔλεγχος also ranges from convince and correct to reprove and punish. With these outcomes, more than their lexical meanings, the second clause with ἔλεγχος is found to be in parallel with the first in appositive relationship, because ὑπόστασις, "confidence" "realization," is supported by and through ἔλεγχος. Therefore, as NIDNTT comments and as TDNT and EDNT also agree, "The purpose of the statement is not so much to encourage subjective assurance of faith, as if faith could give the status of reality to what lies in the future. It is rather to secure a firm link with objectivity" (s.v. ἔλεγχος).

B. καί and ἀλλά

If there are two Greek words that almost no Greek students would be able to forget their meanings for they are frequently used in any Greek text. However, not every Greek student knows these basic words may perform special functions when they are used in the beginning of a sentence. Indeed their frequency is often reverted when they appear in the beginning of a sentence as a rhetorical exclaimer: "well," "now," "behold," etc. Most English translations translate them awkwardly as "and" or "but" even when they are in the first place of a sentence. Thus, the final definition of a word in the Bible is given by a sound theology with humble and critical mind in prayerful spirit.

C. Too many examples

Inevitably translations can only give the best that their languages can hold transferring meanings. Thus, when some words, concepts, ideas, grammars and other features are not available in their languages some words can never be accurately and fully translated. For example, no translation can give good answers why Paul and Barnabas departed, why Herod cut John's head risking his reputation, what was in the mind of Pilate when he was washing his hands before Jesus and so on. But the Greek New Testament readily informs and verifies the answers for these questions.

IV. "Almost" Same

A. Humility

One of the most loved verses in the Bible is found in Philippians 4:4-7. However, if one reads them carefully they should realize they make little sense. In v. 4 Paul tells them to "rejoice" with much emphasis, but then in the next verse he commands them to show their gentleness (or, kindness, humility, or even mercy) to others. Then he also warns (?) them that the Lord is near in the same verse. How can one rejoice, be humble, and be warned at the same time? In fact the answer is found in the Greek text. The word gentleness ἐπιεικές has a restricted implication for divine nature. On the contrary there is another word in the same meaning for humans, namely ταπεινός that is used in James 4:10. With this new knowledge it is a little surprise that Paul says to show (God's) gentleness in association with him (for God is near).

B. Love

There is only one occasion that Jesus asks anyone if he loves Him. In John 21:15-17 Jesus asks Peter "ἀγαπᾷς με;" twice (vv. 15f), but then the third time in v. 17 Jesus asks he says "φιλεῖς με;" Pastors can be easily tempted to over-spiritualize their difference; nevertheless, such attempt is not only wrong but also dangerous because it often makes listeners to consider God's message out of context. In fact the difference between two words is insignificant that the switch of words only gives rhetorical value. For this reason, an exegetical understanding of the text must induce (not deduce) a homiletical one.

C. Power and Energy

Another example of insignificant difference can be illustrated from two words, δύναμις and ἐνέργεια. Most of them they are used interchangeably to mean power or energy. However, sometimes they may intend to show a subtle difference. For example, in Rom 1:16 Paul seems to choose δύναμις over ἐνέργεια in order to denote God's authoritative power (i.e. authority) for the salvation of mankind; however, in Eph 2:12 Paul seems to prefer ἐνέργεια over δύναμις in order to depict God's active power (i.e. energy) rather than his authority.

D. To Reveal

There is a subtle distinction between two words to mean "to reveal": ἀποκαλύπτω and φαίνω. They can be used interchangeably but Paul tends to use them distinctively. The former to mean a divine revelation, which is often unrecognized by man, but the latter is to mean a sign or revelation that is supposed to be understood even by man.

E. Witness

Another two words with "almost" same meaning are δοκίμιον and μαρτύριον. They can simple mean "testimony" or "witness." However, if one understand the difference between the English words "proof" and "evidence" δοκίμιον and μαρτύριον too may claim a slight difference. As the English word "proof" denotes a proven fact and "evidence" a untested (not yet proven) reality, δοκίμιον and μαρτύριον means different. The former requires testing and active participation in order to show its factuality, and thus, often translated to mean "test." But the latter always means witness, testimony for it is either assumed to be factual or does not require testing.

V. Fallacy

G. K. Chesterton once said that all roads led to Rome and that was the very reason only few people got to Rome. This paradoxical insight is also true in the vocabulary study. The following words are common that not enough students ever question their true meanings.

A. μονογενῆ

This is probably one of the most misunderstood—yet theologically significant—words in the Bible along with ἐκκλησία, ἀπόστολος and ἁμαρτία. Only because μόνος is compounded γίνομαι it cannot be construed as "only-begotten" like KJV and NASB. It is like saying the word "butterfly" is originated from a fly which likes butter, that which is epistemology-cally untrue. Neither μονογηνῆ should not be translated as just "only" (ESV) or even "one and only" (NIV, NET, HCSB, MSG). While the rendering "one and only" sound close it is still vague when it is juxtaposed with the fact that believers are *also* called to become his sons. BDAG explicates the use of μονογηνῆ in John 3:16 as, "pertaining to being the only one of its kind, *unique*." For this reason, the reading "unique" is the only possible one for μονογηνῆ in that τὸν υἱὸν τὸν μονογηνῆ denotes a unique son, a son like the unique father himself. It is also stunning to realize that the same expression is first used of Issac the unique—not *only*—child of Abraham (cf. Gen 22:2, 12): יְחִידְךָ-אֶת בִּנְךָ-אֶת (cf. PGG, 342f).

B. δοῦλος

This word means a slave and there is no argument
about it. However, it is its context that sometimes adds
a special rendering for this word. For example, in the
beginning of an epistle the apostle Paul often introduces
himself as δοῦλος Χριστοῦ *the slave of Christ*, and
most readers usually consider it as Paul's humble
expression of himself. However, unlike what many
people often consider this phrase it is quite far from an
expression of humility, but an authority. It is true that
δοῦλος means a slave, but it is also true that it is used to
express an authoritative position of special servant with
a divine calling such as an apostle.

C. ἀπόστολος

The word ἀπόστολος has a lexical meaning an apostle,
but this meanings nothing unless one knows what it
apostle means. Whatever it means at least, it does not
mean "one who is sent" as many have been wrongly
told. There is a cognate verb *ἀποστέλλω* with a meaning
to send forth, or to dismiss. However, this cannot
automatically warrant the meaning of ἀπόστολος being
one who is sent. Etymologically speaking is not found
before the New Testament writings; morphologically
speaking the ending –ολος does not give right to form
an agent (noun); theologically speaking, the apostles
are only limited to those who has witnessed the risen
Christ, and no one since then can be called as such
unlike some ministers like to refer themselves even in
present day. Therefore, ἀπόστολος is rather a
messenger or a special messanger with a divine calling.

VI. Transfooled!

Does theology for everyone? Yes. There is no doubt about that since God commands man to know and build relationship with Him. Theology opens the very first door for it through the Bible. Then, where do many believers build their own theology? The answer should be through the daily reading and study of the Bible, but more likely present age may find their answers from pastors and their sermons. But then, what if the pastors too busy to read the Bible and they too rely their theology from their seminary professors and their books? Disastrous!

Philippians 4:5
One of the most loved passages in the Bible is Philippians 4:4-7. Strangely enough, however, the readers of the passage do not seem to question or throw a doubt on how rejoicing χαίρετε in the verse 4 and gentleness ἐπεεικές in the next verse can make a natural flow of sense. A popular way of preaching this passage is to give an eschatological answer for this saying that the Lord is near (in order to punish otherwise) from verse 5b. However, no satisfactory answer can be given unless one looks up a lexicon and find ἐπεεικές is means the gentleness *of God*. Therefore, Paul commands believers to rejoice (v. 4) and share divine gentleness to others (v. 5a) through the indwelling of the Lord (v. 5b).

Please write your own experience to be transfooled.

VII. References

A. Overview

Eugene Peterson gives an interesting interpretion for Matthew 12:34 in the Message: "It is your heart, not the dictionary, that gives meaning to your words." It is not only a superb interpretation but also theologically sound one as well. In this last chapter of PGV the current author wishes to remind the students that lexicons are authoritative means as a reference but not the referential authority. Final meaning of a word should be deduced from more than one source; the final meaning of a word must be an integrative outcome of various references including lexicons such as BDAG.

B. How to read a lexicon

Basic knowledge for reading a lexicon.

> δοῦλος, ου, ὁ, nom. sg. m. n. *enslaved*; as a subst. *a slave.*

= The article ὁ indicates it is a masculine noun with its genitive form δοῦλ-ου.

> καλέω, ῶ, fut. καλῶ or καλῆσω, aor. ἐκάλεσα, perf. pass. κέκλημαι, aor. pass. ἐκλήθην *to call.*

= The ῶ tells it is an active indicative with different tenses.

> ἀγαθός, ή, όν, nom. sg. m. adj., *good, profitable,*

= Having the two extra ending forms indicates that it is an adjective with the masculine (ἀγαθός), feminine (ἀγαθή), and neuter (ἀγαθόν) forms.

C. Selected Lexicons and Word Study References

Balz, Horst, and Gerhard Schneider, eds. *Exegetical Dictionary of the New Testament.* 3 vols. Grand Rapids: Eerdmans, 1978-80. [EDNT].

Bauer, Walter. *A Greek-English Lexicon of the New Testament and Other Early Christian Literature.* Trans., W. F. Arndt and F. W. Gingrich; 2nd ed. Augmented F. W. Gingrich and F. W. Danker. Chicago: University of Chicago, 1979.

Brown, Colin, ed. *The New International Dictionary of the New Testament Theology.* 3 vols. Grand Rapids: Zondervan, 1986. [NIDNTT].

Danker, Frederick William, rev. ed. *A Greek-English Lexicon of the New Testament and Other Early Christian Literature.* 3rd ed. Based on Walter Bauer's *Griechisch-deutsches Wörterbuch zu den Schriften des Neuen Testaments und der fröhchristlichen Literatur,* 6th ed., ed. Kurt Aland and Barbara Aland, with Viktor Reichmann and on previous English Editions by W. F. Arndt, F. W. Gingrich, and F. W. Danker. Chicago: University of Chicago Press, 2000. [BDAG].

Kittel, Gerhard, and G. Friedrich, eds. *Theological Dictionary of the New Testament.* 10 vols. Trans. Geoffrey W. Bromiley. Grand Rapids: Eerdmans 1964-74. [TDNT].

Liddell, Henry George, and Robert Scott. *A Greek-English Lexicon.* New ed., H. S. Jones, et al. Oxford: Clarendon, 1940 + Barber, E. A. et al. *Supplement.* 1968.

Louw, Johannes P., and Eugene A. Nida, eds. *Greek-English Lexicon of the New Testament Based on Semantic Domains.* 2nd ed. 2 vols. New York: United Bible Societies, 1989. [Louw].

Mounce, William D. *The Analytical Lexicon to the Greek New Testament.* Zondervan Greek Reference Series. Grand Rapids: Zondervan, 1993.

Perschbacher, Wesley J, ed. *The Analytical Greek Lexicon.* Peabody, MA: Hendrickson, 1990.

Trenchard, Warren C. *Complete Vocabulary Guide to the Greek New Testament.* Rev. ed. Grand Rapids: Zondervan, 1998.

__________. *A Concise Dictionary of New Testament Greek.* Cambridge: Cambridge University Press, 2003.

Wilson, Mark, and Jason Oden. *Mastering New Testament Greek Vocabulary Through Semantic Domains.* Grand Rapids: Kregel, 2003.

Study Note

Study Note

MAY GOD BLESS YOUR SERVICE FOR THE LORD

What Some Reviewers Say about
Progressive Greek Grammar

"Unique and Inspiring!"

> \- Jacob Harrison

"Finally, a grammar that is actually useful for building sermons has arrived."

> \- Pastors' Weekly Forum, N.E.X.T.

"I can see Jung's method replacing much of the way Greek is taught today."

> \- Bryan Beach

"I recommend his method to anyone who has a hunger for the Word of God and a passion to see godliness and sanctification developed in his life."

> \- Alyssa Conner

"The book makes studying the Greek language fun and exciting while simultaneously offering its students a book that is academically challenging."

> \- Josiah Durfee

"I would recommend it to anyone like me who has a fear for learning Greek."

> \- Rachel Williams

"As a pastor, PGG leads me to study the Bible to find God's will and mind."

> \- ByungSung Kim

"Difficulty is finally overcomed by difference."
- James C. Lee

"Jung's heart is for anyone to learn Greek and that's what PGG accomplishes"
- Jake Sizemore

"Stellar work by a godly man...this book shouts to the student that learning Biblical Greek is a grand spiritual privilege, not solely an academic venture"
- Trevor Hanson

"As the first book on the Progressive Series PGG is a great place to start."
- H. W. Lee

"Contagious Passion...the book convinced me of its timeless usefulness and practicality. "
- Adam Kent

"Different, not difficult. It's all Greek to me, and I am comfortable with it."
- Jennifer Hill

"Written by a non-native Greek professor, who understands pain of learning a new language."
- Jessica Lim

Thank you and may the Lord bless your study!